Stacy A Stephens

REAL ESTATE
FINANCING
INVESTING

A Complete Guide

CONTENTS

The Power of Real Estate Investing and Financing

Real estate has long been one of the most reliable pathways to wealth, offering a mix of appreciation, cash flow, and tax benefits that few other investments can match. Whether you're a new investor looking to buy your first property or a seasoned pro seeking to expand your portfolio, financing is a critical part of the journey. Financing doesn't just enable you to purchase property; it empowers you to leverage your resources, maximize returns, and build wealth over time. Understanding the ins and outs of real estate financing is essential to making smart, profitable investments.

This Book is designed to demystify real estate financing and give you the insights and tools needed to make informed decisions. From learning about different types of properties and their financing options to grasping the calculations underwriters use, each chapter is packed with practical advice, real-world examples, and expert insights. Financing can feel complex, but it doesn't have to be intimidating. With the right knowledge, you'll be equipped to navigate the process confidently, leveraging the best financing options for each unique investment.

Who This Book Is For

This book is for real estate investors at all levels, from the aspiring home flipper to the commercial property buyer. If you're looking to understand financing options, get a handle on what underwriters look for, or learn how to calculate important metrics like Loan-to-Value Ratio (LTV) and Debt-Service Coverage Ratio (DSCR), this guide is for you. By the end, you'll not only understand financing options, but you'll also have the tools to create a financing strategy aligned with your goals.

What You'll Learn

In the chapters that follow, we'll break down the world of real estate financing in clear, actionable terms:

- Property Classifications and How They're Financed: Understand the differences between residential, commercial, and mixed-use properties, and learn the financing methods that best suit each type.
- Loan Types and Qualification Criteria: Discover the variety of loans available— from traditional mortgages to private loans —and the requirements to qualify.
- Underwriting Insights: Dive into the key factors underwriters evaluate, from credit scores to cash reserves, so you can present a strong application.
- Essential Calculations: Master calculations like DSCR and NOI to evaluate potential investments and make sound financial decisions.

Each section builds on the last, ensuring that by the time you reach the end of this guide, you're equipped with a comprehensive understanding of how real estate financing works and how to use it to achieve your investment goals.

Your Journey Starts Here

Building wealth through real estate is a powerful way to secure your financial future, but it's not without challenges. This Book is your roadmap, providing the knowledge you need to approach financing strategically and confidently. No matter where you are in your real estate journey, you'll find tools and strategies here to help you make informed, profitable financing decisions that can lead to financial freedom. Let's dive in and unlock the potential of real estate investing together.

Understanding Property Classifications

Real estate is a diverse asset class, encompassing a variety of property types that serve different purposes and require different investment strategies. Before diving into the financing details, it's essential to understand the fundamental property classifications within real estate investing. These classifications—residential, commercial, mixed-use, and specialty properties—dictate not only the type of loan you might qualify for but also the potential returns and risks associated with each type.

In this chapter, we'll explore these primary property types, their unique characteristics, and how they align with different investment goals. By the end, you'll have a clearer understanding of which property type may best fit your investment objectives.

1.1 Residential Properties

Overview

Residential properties are designed primarily for individuals or families to live in. This category includes single-family homes, townhouses, condominiums, and multi-family units up to four units (e.g., duplexes, triplexes, and fourplexes). For most investors, residential properties are attractive because they are relatively straightforward to finance and manage, making them an ideal starting point for new real estate investors.

Financing Options

Financing for residential properties tends to be more accessible and affordable, particularly for properties with one to four units. Conventional loans, FHA loans, and VA loans are commonly used, especially when the investor plans to live in one unit of a multi-family property (a strategy known as "house hacking").

- Conventional Loans: These are typically available for properties with 1–4 units. Lenders often require a down payment of 15–25% for investment properties.
- FHA Loans: These loans are an option for 1–4 unit properties if the buyer intends to live in one unit. Down payments start as low as 3.5% with qualifying credit scores.
- VA Loans: Eligible veterans can use VA loans to buy up to a four-unit property with no down payment, as long as one unit is their primary residence.

Advantages and Risks

Residential properties offer predictable cash flow, lower entry costs, and typically higher liquidity, meaning they can be sold more quickly than commercial properties. However, they may yield lower returns than some commercial investments, and their value is often tied closely to local housing market trends.

Understanding Property Classifications

1.2 Commercial Properties

Overview

Commercial properties are primarily used for business purposes and encompass a wide range of buildings, from retail spaces and office buildings to warehouses and multi-family properties with five or more units. Investors are often drawn to commercial properties because they tend to generate higher rental income and are often backed by long-term leases.

Types of Commercial Properties

- Multi-family (5+ units): Apartment buildings and complexes.
- Office Buildings: Ranging from single-story offices to multi-story buildings.
- Retail Spaces: Includes shopping centers, storefronts, and malls.
- Industrial: Warehouses, manufacturing spaces, and distribution centers.
- Specialty: Hotels, medical facilities, and self-storage units.

Financing Options

Financing commercial properties is generally more complex than residential. Lenders rely heavily on the income potential of the property, requiring a Debt Service Coverage Ratio (DSCR) of 1.25 or higher. Common financing options include:

- Commercial Mortgages: Requires a higher down payment (often 20–30%) and generally shorter loan terms than residential loans.
- SBA Loans: For small businesses investing in commercial real estate, SBA 504 and 7(a) loans offer favorable terms.
- DSCR Loans: These loans assess the property's income potential and are ideal for investors who want to qualify based on the property's cash flow.

Advantages and Risks

Commercial properties offer higher income potential, tenant diversity, and often longer lease terms. However, they also involve more considerable upfront investment, complex management requirements, and greater exposure to economic shifts affecting business tenants.

Understanding Property Classifications

1.3 Mixed-Use Properties

Overview

Mixed-use properties combine residential and commercial elements in a single building or complex. A common example might be a building with retail shops on the ground floor and residential units above. This type of property is appealing to investors seeking to diversify income streams within a single investment.

Financing Options

Financing a mixed-use property can be more complicated since it falls between residential and commercial property categories. Lenders will typically evaluate the dominant use (residential vs. commercial) to determine the type of financing:

- Commercial Loans: Often preferred for mixed-use properties, particularly when the property includes significant commercial space.
- Conventional Loans: May be available if the residential portion is dominant and the property has 4 or fewer units.
- FHA Loans: Can be used if the property is mostly residential (1–4 units) and the investor lives in one unit.

Advantages and Risks

Mixed-use properties allow for diversification within a single asset and can help reduce vacancy risk. However, the management and leasing of these properties are often more complex, and they may be affected by both residential and commercial market trends.

Understanding Property Classifications

1.4 Specialty Properties

Overview

Specialty properties encompass unique investments that don't fit neatly into other categories. These can include short-term rentals, hotels, self-storage facilities, medical offices, and senior housing. Specialty properties often require specialized knowledge and have unique financing and regulatory requirements.

Types of Specialty Properties

- Short-Term Rentals: Residential properties rented out for short stays, like vacation rentals.
- Hotels and Motels: Accommodations rented on a nightly basis.
- Self-Storage Facilities: Often found in suburban and industrial areas.
- Senior Housing and Assisted Living: Requires experience in healthcare and often falls under specific regulations.

Financing Options

Financing for specialty properties is often customized and may require higher down payments and a clear business plan. Common options include:

- Commercial Loans: Suitable for specialty properties with business income, such as hotels and storage facilities.
- Hard Money Loans: For short-term, high-return properties like vacation rentals or properties with planned renovations.
- Private Loans: For niche or unconventional properties not easily financed through traditional lenders.

Advantages and Risks

Specialty properties can be highly lucrative, often benefiting from unique demand in their market niche. However, they require specialized management and are subject to market volatility and regulatory challenges.

Understanding Property Classifications

1.5 Choosing the Right Property Type for Your Investment Goals

Understanding the nuances of different property types is key to choosing the right investment strategy. Ask yourself the following questions as you evaluate your options:

- What is my risk tolerance? Residential properties generally have lower risk, while commercial and specialty properties may have higher rewards but come with increased complexity.
- How involved do I want to be in management? Commercial and mixed-use properties may require more hands-on or specialized management, while residential properties may be easier to outsource.
- What are my financing options? Residential properties have more financing options, while commercial and specialty properties often require higher down payments and may involve more complex qualification requirements.

Property classification is the foundation of your investment strategy, influencing everything from financing options to management style and long-term returns. Each property type has unique characteristics, risks, and rewards, and understanding these distinctions will help you make well-informed investment decisions. In the next chapter, we'll dive into the variety of loan types available for each property category, helping you align your financing strategy with your chosen property type.

Types of Real Estate Investment Loans

Financing is a crucial part of real estate investing. The right loan can open doors to profitable opportunities, while the wrong one can add undue risk and limit your investment's potential. In this chapter, we'll explore the primary types of loans available to real estate investors, including their key features, eligibility criteria, and ideal use cases. By the end, you'll have a solid understanding of which loan types are best suited to different property classifications and investment goals.

2.1 Conventional Loans

Overview

Conventional loans are standard mortgages provided by private lenders, including banks, credit unions, and mortgage companies. These loans are not backed by government programs and often come with stricter qualification requirements. Conventional loans are popular for both primary residences and investment properties, particularly for investors seeking long-term financing for residential properties.

Key Features

- Fixed or adjustable interest rates
- Loan terms usually range from 15 to 30 years
- Requires a down payment, often 15–25% for investment properties
- Typically has lower rates than non-conventional loans if credit and income meet high standards

Eligibility Criteria

- Credit Score: Generally 620+ for investment properties
- Debt-to-Income Ratio (DTI): Lenders typically require a DTI of 43% or lower
- Down Payment: Minimum 15–25% for investment properties
- Income Verification: Full documentation of income, assets, and employment

Ideal Use Cases

Conventional loans are well-suited for investors who meet strong credit and income requirements and plan to hold a property long-term. They work best for single-family homes and smaller multi-family units (up to four units).

Types of Real Estate Investment Loans

2.2 FHA Loans

Overview

FHA loans are mortgages insured by the Federal Housing Administration. Although primarily designed for primary residences, FHA loans can be used for investment properties if the borrower lives in one of the units, making them a viable option for investors interested in multi-family properties with up to four units.

Key Features

- Low down payment requirement (as low as 3.5%)
- Fixed and adjustable rate options available
- Can be assumable, meaning a buyer can take over the loan in the future

Eligibility Criteria

- Credit Score: Minimum 580 with a 3.5% down payment; 500 with 10% down
- Occupancy Requirement: Borrower must occupy one of the units
- Debt-to-Income Ratio (DTI): Maximum DTI ratio of 43%
- Property Standards: Must meet FHA property standards

Ideal Use Cases

FHA loans are ideal for "house hacking," where an investor buys a multi-family property, lives in one unit, and rents out the others to offset mortgage costs. This strategy can be a smart entry point into real estate investing for those with limited capital.

Types of Real Estate Investment Loans

2.3 VA Loans

Overview

VA loans are a benefit for active-duty military members, veterans, and eligible spouses, provided by private lenders but backed by the Department of Veterans Affairs. While VA loans are primarily designed for primary residences, they can be used for investment purposes if the borrower lives in one of the units in a multi-family property (up to four units).

Key Features

- No down payment requirement
- Competitive interest rates with no private mortgage insurance (PMI)
- Flexible credit requirements

Eligibility Criteria

- Service Requirements: Must meet specific military service criteria
- Occupancy Requirement: Borrower must occupy one of the units
- Property Requirements: Limited to 1–4 unit properties if used for investment purposes

Ideal Use Cases

VA loans are advantageous for eligible veterans and service members looking to invest in a multi-family property while living in one unit, providing an affordable pathway to homeownership and investment.

Types of Real Estate Investment Loans

2.4 DSCR Loans

Overview

Debt Service Coverage Ratio (DSCR) loans are designed specifically for investment properties and allow investors to qualify based on the income generated by the property rather than personal income. DSCR loans are popular among experienced investors with strong cash-flowing properties.

Key Features

- No personal income verification required
- Qualification based on the DSCR, which measures the property's cash flow relative to debt payments
- Typically requires a higher down payment

Eligibility Criteria

- DSCR Requirement: Minimum DSCR of 1.2 to 1.25, depending on the lender
- Down Payment: 20–30% depending on credit profile and property type
- Credit Score: Minimum 620, though some lenders may have higher requirements

Ideal Use Cases

DSCR loans are ideal for investors with rental properties that generate consistent cash flow, particularly those who have multiple investment properties or prefer to qualify based on property performance rather than personal income.

Types of Real Estate Investment Loans

2.5 Hard Money Loans

Overview

Hard money loans are short-term loans backed by private investors or companies rather than traditional banks. These loans are typically used by investors who need fast funding, often for fix-and-flip projects or properties that may not qualify for conventional financing.

Key Features
- Short loan terms (typically 6 to 36 months)
- Higher interest rates than conventional loans
- Collateral-focused, with loan amounts based on property value

Eligibility Criteria
- Loan-to-Value Ratio (LTV): Often capped at 70-80% of property value
- Experience: Many lenders prefer borrowers with a track record in real estate investing, especially for fix-and-flip projects
- Property Condition: Properties need to have potential value upon renovation or development

Ideal Use Cases

Hard money loans are an excellent option for investors focused on short-term real estate deals, such as property flipping, where quick access to capital is more important than low interest rates.

Types of Real Estate Investment Loans

2.6 Commercial Loans

Overview

Commercial loans are designed for properties with five or more units or for non-residential real estate investments. These loans are usually structured differently from residential loans, often with shorter terms and a focus on the property's income potential rather than the borrower's personal finances.

Key Features

- Higher down payment requirements (typically 20–30%)
- Loan terms of 5, 10, or 15 years with a balloon payment or amortization over 25–30 years
- Rates and terms often influenced by the property's performance metrics (DSCR, NOI)

Eligibility Criteria

- Debt Service Coverage Ratio (DSCR): Generally requires a DSCR of 1.25 or higher
- Loan-to-Value Ratio (LTV): Typically capped at 75–80%
- Credit Score: Minimum of 650, though higher scores improve terms

Ideal Use Cases

Commercial loans are ideal for investors purchasing larger multi-family units, office spaces, retail buildings, or industrial properties where the property's income potential is a key consideration.

Types of Real Estate Investment Loans

2.7 Bridge Loans

Overview

Bridge loans are short-term financing solutions used to "bridge" the gap between buying a property and securing long-term financing. They are frequently used in situations where an investor needs to close quickly or in cases where the property needs significant renovation before qualifying for a traditional loan.

Key Features
- Short loan terms, usually 6 to 18 months
- High interest rates due to short term and risk profile
- Often used for properties undergoing renovation or pending sale

Eligibility Criteria
- Equity in Property: Lenders typically require equity or a strong business plan
- Exit Strategy: Clear plan for repayment, usually through refinancing or sale

Ideal Use Cases

Bridge loans are ideal for investors who need to close deals quickly or who plan to improve and refinance or sell the property within a short time frame.

Types of Real Estate Investment Loans

2.7 Bridge Loans

Overview

Bridge loans are short-term financing solutions used to "bridge" the gap between buying a property and securing long-term financing. They are frequently used in situations where an investor needs to close quickly or in cases where the property needs significant renovation before qualifying for a traditional loan.

Key Features

- Short loan terms, usually 6 to 18 months
- High interest rates due to short term and risk profile
- Often used for properties undergoing renovation or pending sale

Eligibility Criteria

- Equity in Property: Lenders typically require equity or a strong business plan
- Exit Strategy: Clear plan for repayment, usually through refinancing or sale

Ideal Use Cases

Bridge loans are ideal for investors who need to close deals quickly or who plan to improve and refinance or sell the property within a short time frame.

Types of Real Estate Investment Loans

2.8 Bank Statement Loans

Overview

Bank statement loans allow borrowers to qualify based on cash flow reflected in their bank statements rather than traditional income documentation. This option is ideal for self-employed investors or those with non-traditional income sources.

Key Features

- Qualification based on 12-24 months of personal or business bank statements
- Higher down payment requirements
- No need for tax returns or W-2s

Eligibility Criteria

- Bank Statements: Typically 12-24 months of consistent deposits required
- Credit Score: Minimum 620, but 700+ is preferred for better rates
- Down Payment: 20-25% depending on credit and property type

Ideal Use Cases

Bank statement loans are well-suited for self-employed investors who have strong cash flow but may not have traditional income documentation.

Selecting the right loan type is a pivotal step in real estate investing. Each loan type offers unique advantages and limitations based on your financial situation, property type, and investment strategy. As you become familiar with these options, you can match loan types to specific property types and goals, giving you a competitive edge in making informed financing decisions.

In the next chapter, we'll delve into how different property types impact financing strategies, providing further insight into choosing the right loan for your investment.

Qualification Requirements for Real Estate Financing

Financing real estate investments requires meeting specific qualification standards that vary by loan type, lender, and property classification. Understanding these requirements helps investors prepare for the application process and increase their chances of approval. In this chapter, we'll cover the essential qualifications lenders seek, including credit score, income documentation, down payments, debt-to-income ratio (DTI), and property eligibility standards. Additionally, we'll explore the differences in qualification requirements across conventional, government-backed, and alternative loan types.

3.1 Credit Score Requirements

Overview

Credit scores play a critical role in real estate financing, as they reflect the investor's ability to manage debt and make timely payments. Lenders consider credit scores to assess the risk associated with lending to a particular borrower, often using higher credit scores as a criterion for better interest rates and loan terms.

Loan Type Standards

- **Conventional Loans**: Typically require a minimum credit score of 620, although scores of 700 or higher are recommended for favorable terms.
- **FHA Loans:** Allow credit scores as low as 580 for those making a minimum 3.5% down payment. Borrowers with scores between 500-579 may still qualify with a 10% down payment.
- **VA Loans:** No official credit score minimum, but most lenders prefer a score of 620 or higher.
- **DSCR Loans** and Bank Statement Loans: Often have more flexible credit score requirements, though a score of 620 or above is generally expected for favorable terms.

Improving Credit for Financing

Investors aiming to qualify for better loan terms should consider building their credit score by reducing outstanding debts, making timely payments, and minimizing hard inquiries on their credit reports before applying.

Qualification Requirements for Real Estate Financing

3.2 Down Payment Requirements

Overview

The down payment is one of the largest upfront costs in real estate investment and can impact both the financing options available and the overall cost of the loan. Higher down payments generally reduce the lender's risk and can improve loan terms.

Loan Type Standards

- **Conventional Loans**: Require a down payment of 15-25% for investment properties, depending on creditworthiness and property type. Owner-occupied properties may require only 3-5%.
- **FHA Loans**: Allow a minimum down payment of 3.5% if the property is owner-occupied.
- **VA Loans**: Eligible veterans may qualify for 100% financing with no down payment on an owner-occupied investment.
- **DSCR Loans**: Typically require 20-30% down, depending on property type and income potential.
- **Hard Money Loans**: Often require 20-30% down due to the higher risk for short-term or fix-and-flip projects.

Strategies to Save for a Down Payment

Investors can leverage savings plans, home equity from other properties, or partner with other investors to meet down payment requirements. Additionally, many financing programs allow cash gifts or grants toward down payments, making them accessible for qualified borrowers.

Qualification Requirements for Real Estate Financing

3.3 Debt-to-Income Ratio (DTI) Requirements

Overview

DTI ratio measures the borrower's total debt payments against their gross monthly income, helping lenders assess the investor's capacity to handle additional debt. Lenders generally prefer low DTI ratios to ensure borrowers can comfortably manage mortgage payments.

Loan Type Standards

- **Conventional Loans:** Aim for a DTI of 36% or lower, though some lenders may accept up to 45% for strong applicants.
- **FHA Loans:** Generally accept a DTI up to 43-50%, depending on credit score and compensating factors.
- **VA Loans:** No specific DTI limit, but lenders commonly expect a DTI of 41% or less.
- **DSCR Loans:** These loans rely more on the property's income than the borrower's DTI, making them a flexible option for investors with high existing debt.
- **Commercial Loans:** DTI is often replaced by the DSCR (Debt Service Coverage Ratio) to measure the property's ability to generate sufficient income to cover debt obligations.

Reducing DTI for Loan Approval

Paying down outstanding debts, refinancing high-interest debts, or increasing monthly income streams can help investors meet DTI requirements for financing approval.

Qualification Requirements for Real Estate Financing

3.4 Income Documentation Requirements

Overview

Lenders typically require income documentation to verify the borrower's ability to repay the loan. This documentation varies by loan type, with conventional loans requiring standard income proof while alternatives like DSCR and bank statement loans allow for flexibility with income verification.

Types of Documentation

- **Conventional Loans:** Require W-2s, tax returns, and pay stubs for income verification.
- **Bank Statement Loans:** Use 12-24 months of bank statements to establish income, ideal for self-employed investors or those with non-traditional income sources.
- **DSCR Loans:** Focus on the property's income rather than the borrower's, reducing the need for personal income documentation.
- **Hard Money Loans:** Generally require minimal income documentation, as these loans are asset-based, focusing on the property's value or the after-repair value (ARV).

Preparation Tips

Investors should gather tax returns, recent bank statements, and income records well in advance to streamline the application process. For self-employed individuals, maintaining well-documented income streams can simplify the qualification process for alternative financing options.

Qualification Requirements for Real Estate Financing

3.5 Property Eligibility Requirements

Overview

Property eligibility standards are a key component of the underwriting process. Lenders assess the property's type, location, condition, and income potential to determine its suitability as collateral for the loan.

Loan Type Standards

- **Conventional Loans:** Often restricted to single-family homes, condos, and 2-4 unit residential properties, with limitations on condition and market location.
- **FHA/VA Loans:** Limited to owner-occupied properties in livable condition.
- **DSCR and Commercial Loans:** Can finance larger multi-family or mixed-use properties, requiring the property to meet income and appraisal standards.
- **Hard Money Loans:** Focus on distressed properties or those requiring rehabilitation, prioritizing the after-repair value.

Ensuring Property Eligibility

Investors should consider pre-inspections to identify any potential issues that might affect eligibility and address them before applying. Working with experienced real estate agents and appraisers can also improve property eligibility outcomes.

Qualification Requirements for Real Estate Financing

3.6 Cash Reserves and Liquidity

Overview

Many lenders require investors to have cash reserves, especially for larger or riskier investments, as a safeguard against potential income disruptions or unforeseen expenses.

Typical Requirements

- **Conventional Loans:** May require reserves equivalent to 3-6 months of mortgage payments.
- **FHA and VA Loans:** Generally do not require reserves unless there are risk factors.
- **Commercial and DSCR Loans:** Often require reserves based on property cash flow and operating expenses (Can be up to 12 months).
- **Hard Money Loans:** May have little to no reserve requirements but tend to compensate with higher interest rates.

Building Cash Reserves

Setting aside funds from monthly rental income, refinancing existing properties, or leveraging other assets can help investors maintain sufficient reserves. Reserves provide a financial cushion that can help mitigate risk and reassure lenders of the investor's stability.

Qualification requirements for real estate financing vary widely depending on loan type, property classification, and investor profile. Knowing what lenders look for in terms of credit score, down payment, DTI, income, and property eligibility can make a significant difference in the application process. By preparing in advance and selecting the loan type that aligns with their financial situation, investors can improve their chances of securing the financing they need to grow their real estate portfolios.

How Underwriters Evaluate Real Estate Investment Loans

Real estate investment loans involve unique underwriting considerations distinct from primary residence or owner-occupied loans. Underwriting for investment properties goes beyond evaluating the borrower's financial health and dives deeply into the property's potential to generate income and cover debt obligations. Understanding how underwriters approach real estate investment loans gives investors insight into the standards they must meet to secure financing.

In this chapter, we'll break down the core aspects of underwriting for investment properties, including borrower qualifications, property evaluation, financial analysis, and risk assessment factors. We'll also examine common hurdles investors face and strategies to improve approval chances.

4.1 The Underwriting Process for Real Estate Investment Loans

Underwriting for real estate investment loans involves a comprehensive risk assessment by the lender to determine if the loan aligns with their standards and policies. Unlike loans for primary residences, investment property loans carry a higher perceived risk for lenders, largely due to reliance on the property's income to cover loan payments.

Underwriters review both the borrower's and property's financial details. They assess whether the borrower has sufficient creditworthiness and stability while also verifying that the property can generate adequate income. The main objective is to ensure the property will perform financially, allowing the investor to comfortably make loan payments.

How Underwriters Evaluate Real Estate Investment Loans

4.2 Key Components of Underwriter Evaluation

1. Borrower Financial Profile

Underwriters begin by evaluating the borrower's financial strength. A solid financial profile reassures the lender of the borrower's reliability, particularly during economic downturns or periods when the property's income may fluctuate.

- **Credit Score and History:** A strong credit score (typically 680 or above) demonstrates the borrower's history of managing debt responsibly. For investment loans, many lenders have stricter credit score requirements compared to owner-occupied loans due to the higher risk involved.

- **Income Documentation:** Traditional income documentation, such as W-2s, tax returns, and pay stubs, is often required. However, for non-traditional income sources (e.g., self-employed investors), bank statement loans or DSCR loans may be more flexible. DSCR loans, for instance, focus on the property's income rather than the borrower's, offering an alternative for investors without W-2 income.

- **Debt-to-Income (DTI) Ratio:** Although DTI ratios are more flexible for investment loans, lenders still consider this metric to ensure borrowers are not over-leveraged. Generally, a DTI below 45% is preferred, but DSCR loans allow for higher ratios since they prioritize property income.

- **Cash Reserves:** Cash reserves are often required as a safeguard, showing the lender that the investor has the financial stability to cover loan payments in case of rental income interruptions. Requirements typically range from 3 to 12 months of reserves, depending on the loan type, property type, and perceived risk.

How Underwriters Evaluate Real Estate Investment Loans

4.2 Key Components of Underwriter Evaluation

2. Property Analysis

The property's financial potential and condition are central to the underwriting process for investment loans, as the asset itself often secures the lender's risk.

- **Appraisal and Market Value:** The underwriter relies on a professional appraisal to determine the property's market value and verify that it aligns with the loan amount. The appraisal often includes a rental schedule to estimate fair market rents, which underwriters use to validate the property's income potential.

- **Income Potential and DSCR (Debt Service Coverage Ratio):** For investment loans, the Debt Service Coverage Ratio (DSCR) is a crucial metric. DSCR is calculated by dividing the property's net operating income (NOI) by the debt payments. A DSCR of 1.25 or higher is typically preferred, meaning the property generates at least 25% more income than needed to cover debt obligations. A higher DSCR indicates a lower risk to the lender, as it provides a cushion against unexpected income fluctuations.

- **Location and Market Trends:** Location impacts the property's long-term income potential. Underwriters consider factors such as local demand, vacancy rates, and market stability to assess whether the property's rental income can be sustained. Properties in high-demand areas or economically stable regions are often viewed more favorably.

- **Condition of the Property:** Properties in good condition have lower maintenance costs, reducing the likelihood of unexpected expenses that could affect the borrower's ability to make loan payments. Some lenders may require repairs or upgrades before closing if the property is in substandard condition.

How Underwriters Evaluate Real Estate Investment Loans

4.2 Key Components of Underwriter Evaluation

3. Loan Structure and Terms

The loan's structure, purpose, and terms are integral to underwriting, as they affect the risk level.

- **Loan-to-Value (LTV) Ratio:** The LTV ratio measures the loan amount relative to the property's appraised value. For investment properties, LTV ratios are generally capped at 75-80%, meaning the investor must contribute a larger down payment. Lower LTV ratios signal less risk to the lender, as they represent a higher borrower equity stake.

- **Purpose of the Loan:** Underwriters differentiate between loans used for property purchases, refinances, or cash-out refinances. Cash-out refinances involve higher risk as they increase leverage on the property, so underwriters may apply more stringent requirements for these loans.

- **Interest Rate Type and Loan Term:** Fixed-rate loans provide stable payments, reducing risk to the lender compared to adjustable-rate mortgages, which can fluctuate over time. Shorter loan terms also tend to be viewed more favorably, as they reduce the lender's long-term exposure.

How Underwriters Evaluate Real Estate Investment Loans

4.3 Key Risk Assessment Factors

Underwriting for investment loans involves a comprehensive risk assessment. Here are the main factors underwriters consider:

- **Creditworthiness and Stability:** Borrowers with a strong credit history, adequate cash reserves, and low DTI ratios are viewed as lower risk. Lenders may offer favorable terms to these borrowers due to their financial reliability.

- **Property Location and Market Demand:** Properties in economically stable areas with high demand are less risky for lenders, as they are more likely to retain or appreciate in value. Underwriters analyze local market conditions, rental demand, and future growth projections.

- **Vacancy Rates and Operating Costs:** High vacancy rates or excessive operating costs can indicate potential cash flow issues, which can impact the borrower's ability to meet loan payments. Underwriters prefer properties with stable occupancy and manageable expenses to ensure consistent income.

- **Exit Strategy for Short-Term Loans:** For short-term loans (e.g., hard money or bridge loans), underwriters evaluate the borrower's exit strategy, such as selling or refinancing. A well-defined exit strategy reduces risk, particularly if the investor plans to refinance into a long-term loan after property improvements.

Important

How Underwriters Evaluate Real Estate Investment Loans

4.4 Common Underwriting Challenges and Solutions

Investors may encounter several challenges during underwriting. Here are common obstacles and solutions:

- **Low Credit Score or High DTI:** For borrowers with credit or DTI challenges, alternatives like DSCR loans, which focus on property income rather than personal income, may offer a solution. Another option is to increase the down payment, improving the LTV ratio.

- **Unfavorable Appraisal Results:** If the property's appraised value falls short, consider negotiating the purchase price or increasing the down payment to reduce the loan amount. Investors may also seek a second opinion from another appraiser.

- **Property Condition Issues:** Properties in poor condition can delay underwriting. Options include addressing major repairs before closing or opting for hard money loans, which typically have more lenient property condition requirements but come with higher interest rates.

- **Income Documentation for Self-Employed Investors:** Self-employed or non-traditional income borrowers may struggle with documentation. Bank statement loans or DSCR loans, which use cash flow rather than income verification, can provide alternative pathways for these investors.

- **Income Documentation for Self-Employed Investors:** Self-employed or non-traditional income borrowers may struggle with documentation. Bank statement loans or DSCR loans, which use cash flow rather than income verification, can provide alternative pathways for these investors.

How Underwriters Evaluate Real Estate Investment Loans

4.4 Common Underwriting Challenges and Solutions

- **Investor don't own a personal residence:** Underwriting an investment property for someone who doesn't own a personal residence but is purchasing a rental property near their current address can raise red flags, often due to concerns that the buyer intends to use the property as a primary residence rather than an investment.

Here are some strategies to overcome this underwriting challenge:

1. **Document Clear Investment Intent**: Show intent to treat the property as a rental through a well-documented investment plan. This can include a lease agreement or a letter of intent from a potential tenant, as well as any market research supporting the rental demand and potential ROI.

2. **Strong Debt-to-Income (DTI) Ratio:** Lenders may be more comfortable if the borrower has a strong DTI ratio, demonstrating that they can afford the property as an investment without needing to live there.

3. **Solid Rental History**: If the borrower has a history of successful rental investments, this could support their case. Even if they haven't owned a property, showing a history of investment management or positive rental history (if applicable) could provide assurance.

4. **Higher Down Payment:** A larger down payment can sometimes make lenders feel more comfortable, as it reduces the lender's risk and indicates the buyer's commitment to the property as an investment.

5. **Higher Reserves:** Demonstrating strong reserves, especially with six months or more of mortgage payments for the investment property, could help the buyer's case, showing they have the financial means to keep the property as a rental.

6. **Detailed Letter of Explanation:** A letter explaining why the buyer intends to keep the property as an investment and detailing their future housing plans (e.g., renting or purchasing a primary residence elsewhere) can help underwriters understand their intent.

7. **Consider Alternate Mortgage Brokers**: Some lenders, especially non-QM (non-qualified mortgage) or portfolio lenders, may be more flexible in their requirements and able to work with investors who don't own primary residences. These steps may improve the chances of approval by alleviating underwriters' concerns over potential occupancy misrepresentation.

How Underwriters Evaluate Real Estate Investment Loans

4.5 Tips for a Smooth Underwriting Process

To improve approval odds and streamline the underwriting process, consider these tips:

- **Organize Documentation:** Gather all required financial documents, including tax returns, bank statements, and income records, well in advance. For DSCR or bank statement loans, prepare proof of rental income or cash flow statements.
- **Maintain Transparency:** Provide accurate and complete information. Lenders appreciate transparency, as it demonstrates reliability and reduces the likelihood of delays due to missing information.
- **Partner with Experienced Professionals:** Real estate agents, mortgage brokers, and financial advisors can anticipate underwriting challenges and guide you through documentation and qualification requirements, helping expedite the process.
- **Consider Pre-Underwriting:** Some lenders offer pre-underwriting services, allowing them to review your application before you submit a formal offer. This proactive approach identifies potential issues early, increasing your chances of a seamless approval.
- **Stay Communicative and Responsive:** Promptly respond to any requests from your lender. Delays in communication can slow the underwriting process and may even jeopardize loan approval.

Underwriting for real estate investment loans is a complex process that balances the borrower's financial strength with the property's income potential and market position. By understanding the factors underwriters evaluate—creditworthiness, income stability, property value, market demand, and loan structure—investors can approach the underwriting process more effectively. Preparing in advance, maintaining accurate documentation, and selecting the right loan type for your property investment goals can streamline underwriting, bringing you closer to successful real estate investment financing.

How Real Estate Investment Financing Calculations Work

The financial calculations underpinning real estate investment financing play a vital role in determining loan eligibility, structuring deals, and projecting profitability. Understanding these calculations helps investors make more informed decisions about property acquisitions, debt structure, and expected returns.

In this chapter, we'll walk through the key calculations that lenders and underwriters use to assess loan eligibility and investment viability, including loan-to-value (LTV), debt service coverage ratio (DSCR), cash flow, and return on investment (ROI). These calculations are essential for understanding the financial mechanics of investment financing and optimizing your portfolio's performance.

5.1 Loan-to-Value (LTV) Ratio

The Loan-to-Value (LTV) ratio is a primary risk assessment tool used by lenders to determine the loan amount relative to the property's value. For investment properties, LTV requirements are often more stringent than those for owner-occupied homes due to the higher perceived risk.

Formula for LTV:

LTV = (Loan Amount / Appraised Property Value) × 100

For example, if you're purchasing an investment property appraised at $400,000 and applying for a loan of $300,000, the LTV ratio would be:

LTV = (300,000 / 400,000) × 100 = 75%

Lenders typically cap LTV for investment properties around 70–80%, meaning you'll need to provide a down payment to cover the remaining percentage. A lower LTV indicates a higher borrower equity stake, which reduces lender risk and can lead to more favorable loan terms.

How Real Estate Investment Financing Calculations Work

5.2 Debt Service Coverage Ratio (DSCR)

The Debt Service Coverage Ratio (DSCR) is a fundamental metric for investment property loans, particularly in commercial or rental property financing. It assesses whether the property generates enough income to cover debt obligations, providing a cushion for the lender.

Formula for DSCR:

$$DSCR = \text{Net Operating Income (NOI)} / \text{Total Debt Service}$$

For instance, if a rental property has an NOI of $120,000 and annual debt payments of $90,000, the DSCR would be:

$$DSCR = \text{Net Operating Income (NOI)} / \text{Total Debt Service}$$

Given the numbers:

$$DSCR = 90,000 / 120,000 = 1.33$$

This means the property's net operating income is 1.33 times its debt obligations.

A DSCR above 1.0 indicates that the property generates more income than required to cover debt, while a DSCR of 1.25 or higher is generally preferred for investment loans. Properties with higher DSCR ratios are seen as lower risk, as they offer better protection against income fluctuations.

How Real Estate Investment Financing Calculations Work

5.3 Cash Flow Calculations

Cash flow represents the amount of net income a property generates after accounting for all expenses, including debt payments. Positive cash flow is essential for building a profitable real estate portfolio, as it allows for reinvestment and helps cover unexpected expenses.

- Cash Flow=Gross Rental Income-Operating Expenses-Debt Payments

For example, if a property generates $150,000 in annual rental income, incurs $30,000 in operating expenses, and requires $90,000 in debt payments, the cash flow would be:

$$Cash\ Flow=150,000-30,000-90,000=30,000$$

A positive cash flow indicates that the property is not only covering expenses but also generating additional income. Investors typically seek properties with stable or increasing cash flow to ensure long-term profitability.

How Real Estate Investment Financing Calculations Work

5.4 Capitalization Rate (Cap Rate)

The Cap Rate is a valuable metric used to evaluate a property's profitability based on its income potential and market value. It's particularly useful when comparing properties or assessing return potential in a specific market.

- **Formula for Cap Rate:**

  Cap Rate = (Net Operating Income (NOI) / Property Value) × 100

This formula helps investors evaluate the potential return on an investment property.

For example, if a property with an NOI of $80,000 is valued at $1,000,000, the Cap Rate would be:

Cap Rate = (Net Operating Income (NOI) / Property Value) × 100

Given the numbers:

Cap Rate = (80,000 / 1,000,000) × 100 = 8%

A higher Cap Rate indicates a potentially higher return but may also reflect increased risk or market volatility. Cap Rates vary widely by location and property type, with prime properties in high-demand areas typically having lower Cap Rates due to their stability and low risk.

How Real Estate Investment Financing Calculations Work

5.5 Return on Investment (ROI)

ROI is a broad measure that assesses the total profitability of an investment relative to the initial capital invested. It accounts for cash flow, appreciation, and tax benefits, providing a comprehensive picture of an investment's performance.

- **Formula for ROI:**

  ROI = (Annual Cash Flow + Appreciation + Tax Benefits) / Initial Investment × 100

This formula helps determine the overall profitability of an investment by considering cash flow, appreciation, and tax benefits relative to the initial investment.

For instance, if an investor puts $100,000 down on a property, earns an annual cash flow of $10,000, sees an appreciation of $5,000, and benefits from $3,000 in tax savings, the ROI would be:

ROI = (Annual Cash Flow + Appreciation + Tax Benefits) / Initial Investment × 100

Given the numbers:

ROI = (10,000 + 5,000 + 3,000) / 100,000 × 100 = 18%

A high ROI suggests a strong return relative to the initial investment. Investors often aim for properties with a high ROI while balancing risk factors, as ROI alone does not account for potential volatility or market changes.

How Real Estate Investment Financing Calculations Work

5.6 Gross Rent Multiplier (GRM)

The Gross Rent Multiplier (GRM) is a simplified ratio that evaluates a property's value in relation to its gross rental income. While it does not consider expenses, it's a quick tool for comparing potential investments or screening properties.

- **Formula for GRM:**

$$\text{GRM} = \text{Property Price} / \text{Annual Gross Rental Income}$$

This formula helps investors evaluate the potential profitability of a rental property by comparing its price to its gross rental income.

For example, if a property is priced at $500,000 and generates $50,000 in annual rental income, the GRM would be:

Given the numbers:

$$\text{GRM} = 500,000 / 50,000 = 10$$

A lower GRM can indicate a more favorable investment, but it should be used alongside other metrics since it doesn't account for expenses or financing.

How Real Estate Investment Financing Calculations Work

5.7 Loan Constant

The Loan Constant is a useful calculation for understanding the true cost of financing, considering both the loan amount and interest rate. It helps investors compare loan costs across different financing options.

- **Formula for Loan Constant:**

Loan Constant = (Annual Debt Service / Loan Principal) × 100

For instance, if an investor takes a $200,000 loan with an annual debt service of $15,000, the Loan Constant would be:

Given the numbers:

Loan Constant = (15,000 / 200,000) × 100 = 7.5%

The Loan Constant helps investors determine if the property's Cap Rate can support the debt, guiding them in deciding if the financing terms are feasible.

How Real Estate Investment Financing Calculations Work

5.8 Commonly Used Calculations in Action: A Real-Life Example

To bring these concepts together, let's examine how an investor might analyze a rental property using these calculations.

1. **Property Overview:** A multi-family property with a purchase price of $500,000, generating $60,000 in annual gross rental income.
2. **Loan Terms:** The investor plans to take a $400,000 loan (80% LTV) with annual debt service payments of $30,000.
3. **Expenses:** Operating expenses amount to $15,000 per year, resulting in an NOI of $45,000.
4. **Key Calculations:**
   - **LTV:** LTV = (400,000 / 500,000) × 100 = 80%
   - **DSCR:** DSCR = 45,000 / 30,000 = 1.5
   - **Cap Rate:** Cap Rate = (45,000 / 500,000) × 100 = 9%
   - **Cash Flow:** Cash Flow = 60,000 – 15,000 – 30,000 = 15,000
   - **ROI (assuming no appreciation or tax benefits):** ROI = (15,000 / 100,000) × 100 = 15%

This example shows how the various metrics can be used to gauge the property's income potential, financing suitability, and long-term return expectations.

Understanding these calculations is essential for successful real estate investing. Metrics like LTV, DSCR, Cap Rate, and ROI provide critical insights into property performance and financing risks. By mastering these calculations, investors can evaluate potential deals more accurately, align financing structures with investment goals, and optimize portfolio performance. Armed with this knowledge, you can approach investment opportunities confidently, making data-driven

Real Estate Investment Financing Scenarios and Examples

Real estate investment financing can be complex, with financing needs that vary significantly depending on the type of property, investment strategy, and loan structure. In this chapter, we'll explore a variety of financing scenarios to demonstrate how investors might structure loans for different types of real estate investments. Each example will illustrate how financing decisions impact cash flow, loan terms, and the overall investment strategy.

6.1 Single-Family Rental Property

Single-family rentals are a popular choice for new real estate investors due to their simplicity and accessibility. Financing for single-family rentals often resembles traditional home financing, but with unique criteria for investment properties.

Scenario:

- **Property Value:** $300,000
- **Down Payment:** 20% ($60,000)
- **Loan Amount:** $240,000
- **Interest Rate:** 5% (fixed)
- **Loan Term:** 30 years
- **Monthly Rent:** $2,000
- **Monthly Operating Expenses:** $500 (including taxes, insurance, and maintenance)

Calculations:

- **Monthly Mortgage Payment: $1,288 (estimated using a 5% rate over 30 years)**
- **Monthly Cash Flow:**
- **Monthly Rent − Operating Expenses − Mortgage Payment = 2,000 − 500 − 1,288 = 212**
- **Debt Service Coverage Ratio (DSCR):**
  1. **Annual Net Operating Income (NOI): (2,000 − 500) × 12 = 18,000**
  2. **Annual Debt Service: 1,288 × 12 = 15,456**
  3. **DSCR: 18,000 / 15,456 = 1.16**

Investment Summary: In this scenario, the investor achieves a positive cash flow of $212 per month, but the DSCR of 1.16 is relatively low. While this property may cover its debt obligations and produce modest cash flow, the investor should weigh the low DSCR against any potential market risks, vacancy periods, or unexpected maintenance costs.

Real Estate Investment Financing Scenarios and Examples

6.3 Fix-and-Flip Investment

Fix-and-flip investors buy properties at a discount, renovate them, and sell them quickly for a profit. Financing for fix-and-flip projects often involves short-term, higher-interest loans, such as hard money loans, due to the short holding period.

Scenario:

- **Purchase Price:** $150,000
- **Rehab Budget:** $50,000
- **After Repair Value (ARV):** $250,000
- **Loan Amount:** 90% of purchase price + 100% of rehab budget = $185,000
- **Interest Rate:** 10% (interest-only)
- **Loan Term:** 1 year (repay upon sale)
- **Estimated Holding Costs:** $12,000 (insurance, property taxes, utilities, etc.)
- **Sales Price:** $250,000

Calculations:

- **Total Investment:** $50,000 (down payment) + $50,000 (rehab) + $12,000 (holding costs) = $112,000
- **Profit:** Sales Price - Total Investment - Interest Payments = 250,000 - 112,000 - 18,500 = 119,500

Investment Summary: This fix-and-flip example illustrates a high potential profit of $119,500, but it comes with higher risk due to the short-term nature of the investment and reliance on market conditions. Hard money loans enable this type of financing by offering quick access to capital, though with a higher interest rate.

Real Estate Investment Financing Scenarios and Examples

6.4 Short-Term Rental Property

Short-term rentals, such as vacation rentals or Airbnb properties, can yield higher income but require specific financing considerations due to their seasonal nature. Some lenders may allow short-term rental income to qualify, but the DSCR and income projections are often evaluated more cautiously.

Scenario:

- **Property Value:** $500,000
- **Down Payment:** 20% ($100,000)
- **Loan Amount:** $400,000
- **Interest Rate:** 5.5%
- **Loan Term:** 30 years
- **Average Monthly Income (after vacancies and management fees):** $4,000 (seasonal average)
- **Monthly Operating Expenses:** $1,000

Calculations:

- **Monthly Mortgage Payment:** $2,271
- Monthly Cash Flow:
  Average Income – Operating Expenses – Mortgage Payment = 4,000 – 1,000 – 2,271 = 729
- DSCR:
  1. Annual NOI: (4,000 – 1,000) × 12 = 36,000
  2. Annual Debt Service: 2,271 × 12 = 27,252
  3. DSCR: 36,000 / 27,252 = 1.32

Investment Summary: This short-term rental scenario provides positive cash flow and a moderate DSCR of 1.32, demonstrating the potential for profitable returns. However, the investor should account for the seasonality and higher management requirements associated with short-term rentals, as these factors can impact the cash flow consistency.

Real Estate Investment Financing Scenarios and Examples

6.5 Commercial Property Investment

Investing in commercial properties, such as office spaces or retail centers, requires specialized financing and careful cash flow analysis. Lenders usually require significant equity and a DSCR of 1.25 or higher.

Scenario:

- **Property Value:** $2,500,000
- **Down Payment:** 30% ($750,000)
- **Loan Amount:** $1,750,000
- **Interest Rate:** 6%
- **Loan Term:** 20 years
- **Monthly Gross Income:** $20,000
- **Monthly Operating Expenses:** $5,000

Calculations:

- **Monthly Mortgage Payment:** Approximately $12,600
- **Monthly Cash Flow:**

Gross Income – Operating Expenses – Mortgage Payment = 20,000 – 5,000 – 12,600 = 2,400

- **DSCR:**
  1. Annual NOI: (20,000 – 5,000) × 12 = 180,000
  2. Annual Debt Service: 12,600 × 12 = 151,200
  3. DSCR: 180,000 / 151,200 = 1.19

Investment Summary: Although this property has a DSCR of 1.19, it's slightly below typical lender requirements for commercial financing, which could limit loan approval or result in higher interest rates. Investors in commercial properties should be prepared for rigorous underwriting and maintain a healthy cash reserve to cover any fluctuations in tenant occupancy.

Real estate investment financing offers flexibility and options for various property types and investment strategies. By understanding these scenarios, investors can better evaluate their financing needs, choose suitable loan products, and assess the potential risks and rewards. In every financing decision, it's essential to analyze cash flow, debt obligations, and the property's ability to generate sufficient income, ensuring each investment aligns with both financial goals and risk tolerance.

Frequently Asked Questions (FAQ)

Real estate investing involves a range of financial strategies and considerations. New and seasoned investors alike often have questions about financing, eligibility, and the nuances of real estate investment loans. This FAQ chapter addresses common inquiries to help clarify essential topics and demystify complex aspects of real estate investment financing.

1. What Types of Loans Are Available for Real Estate Investors?
Several types of loans cater to different investment needs:

- **Conventional Loans:** Often used for single-family rental properties, these loans require a higher credit score and larger down payment for investment properties than for primary residences.
- **Commercial Real Estate Loans:** Used for multi-family properties with five or more units, office spaces, retail centers, and industrial buildings, these loans typically have shorter terms and higher interest rates.
- **DSCR (Debt Service Coverage Ratio) Loans:** These loans qualify based on the property's rental income rather than the borrower's personal income, ideal for investors who may not meet traditional income documentation requirements.
- **Hard Money Loans:** Short-term loans with higher interest rates, often used by fix-and-flip investors who need quick access to funding.
- **FHA/VA Loans:** Available for primary residences but can sometimes be used for investment purposes if the investor plans to live in one unit of a multi-family property.

2. How Much Down Payment Do I Need for an Investment Property?
Down payment requirements vary based on the loan type, property type, and lender policies. Typically:

- **Single-family rental:** 15-25% down payment
- **Multi-family property (2-4 units):** 20-30% down payment
- **Commercial properties:** 25-35% down payment

Lenders generally require higher down payments for investment properties due to the increased risk compared to owner-occupied homes.

Frequently Asked Questions (FAQ)

3. What Credit Score Do I Need to Qualify for a Real Estate Investment Loan?

Credit score requirements vary by lender and loan product:

- **Conventional loans:** Generally require a minimum credit score of 620–680, though higher scores are preferred for better rates.
- **DSCR and asset-based loans:** Minimum credit scores can range from 620 to 700, depending on the lender.
- **Hard money loans:** Credit requirements may be more flexible, with some lenders accepting scores as low as 550. However, lower credit scores may result in higher interest rates.

4. Can I Use Rental Income to Qualify for a Loan?

Yes, many lenders allow investors to use projected rental income as part of their income qualification. **DSCR loans**, in particular, are based on the property's income-generating potential, making them popular among real estate investors. For conventional loans, lenders often use a percentage of expected rental income from the property to calculate eligibility.

5. What Is a Debt Service Coverage Ratio (DSCR) Loan?

A DSCR loan is a type of financing that relies on the property's rental income to qualify rather than the borrower's personal income. DSCR is a metric used to assess whether the property's income is sufficient to cover debt obligations. DSCR loans are ideal for investors with complex financial profiles or inconsistent income streams who may not qualify for traditional loans.

6. What Is the Loan-to-Value (LTV) Ratio, and Why Does It Matter?

The Loan-to-Value (LTV) ratio is the ratio of the loan amount to the property's appraised value. It's used to assess the risk of the loan; a lower LTV means the borrower has more equity in the property, reducing risk for the lender. For investment properties, LTV ratios usually max out at 70–80%, whereas owner-occupied homes may have higher LTV limits.

Frequently Asked Questions (FAQ)

7. Are Interest Rates Higher for Investment Properties?

Yes, interest rates for investment properties are generally higher than for primary residences. Lenders view investment properties as higher risk due to the potential for vacancies, market fluctuations, and other factors impacting cash flow. Rates may vary based on the borrower's credit score, loan type, down payment, and property type.

8. Can I Refinance an Investment Property to Cash Out Equity?

Yes, investors can refinance an investment property to access its equity, known as a cash-out refinance. This strategy can provide funds for additional investments, renovations, or other financial needs. However, cash-out refinance rates are often higher, and lenders typically require a lower LTV (such as 75-80%) for cash-out refinancing on investment properties.

9. How Do Fix-and-Flip Loans Work?

Fix-and-flip loans are short-term financing solutions, often provided by hard money lenders, designed for investors looking to purchase, renovate, and resell properties quickly. These loans usually have higher interest rates, shorter terms (6-24 months), and require a detailed renovation plan. Fix-and-flip loans focus on the property's ARV (After Repair Value) to assess loan eligibility.

10. What Are the Risks of Real Estate Investment Financing?

Some of the primary risks include:

- **Interest Rate Fluctuations:** Variable rates can lead to unpredictable monthly payments.
- **Vacancies**: Extended vacancies impact cash flow and can strain an investor's ability to meet debt obligations.
- **Property Depreciation:** Market downturns can decrease property values, impacting equity and resale value.
- **Maintenance and Repairs:** Unexpected repairs can reduce profits and create financial strain, particularly for highly leveraged properties.

Frequently Asked Questions (FAQ)

11. How Long Does It Take to Get Financing for an Investment Property?

The timeline varies based on the loan type and lender. Conventional and DSCR loans typically take 30–45 days, while hard money loans can be processed in as little as 1–2 weeks due to their streamlined underwriting process. The complexity of the borrower's financial profile and the lender's due diligence requirements may affect processing times.

12. Can I Get a Loan with No Income Verification?

Yes, several loan products cater to investors without traditional income documentation:

- DSCR Loans: Qualification is based on the property's rental income rather than personal income.
- Bank Statement Loans: These loans use business or personal bank statements to determine income, often used by self-employed borrowers.
- Asset-Based Loans: Qualification is based on the borrower's assets rather than income, though terms may vary based on lender requirements.

13. What Is the Difference Between Hard Money Loans and Conventional Loans?

The primary differences include:

- Interest Rates: Hard money loans typically have higher interest rates (8–15%) compared to conventional loans.
- Term Length: Hard money loans are short-term (6–24 months), while conventional loans usually have 15- to 30-year terms.
- Qualification Criteria: Hard money lenders focus on the property's value and the borrower's exit strategy, whereas conventional lenders review credit scores, income, and other traditional metrics.

14. What Are Points, and How Do They Affect Loan Costs?

Points, or discount points, are upfront fees paid to lower the loan's interest rate. One point typically costs 1% of the loan amount. For example, one point on a $200,000 loan would cost $2,000. Paying points can reduce the monthly payment but increases the initial cost, so investors should weigh the long-term savings against the upfront expense.

Frequently Asked Questions (FAQ)

15. Can I Use My Self-Directed IRA to Invest in Real Estate?

Yes, a self-directed IRA allows for alternative investments, including real estate. However, strict rules apply, including prohibitions on personal use and self-dealing. Investors should work with an IRA custodian familiar with real estate investments to ensure compliance with IRS guidelines.

16. How Is the Property's Value Assessed for a Loan?

Lenders typically order an independent appraisal to determine the property's current market value. For investment properties, appraisals may include an analysis of comparable properties, rental income, and market trends. This valuation is essential in calculating the LTV and determining loan terms.

17. Can I Finance Repairs and Renovations with the Loan?

Yes, some loans—particularly fix-and-flip and renovation loans—allow financing for repairs and renovations. For example, FHA 203(k) loans for owner-occupied properties and certain hard money or bridge loans provide funds based on the property's ARV, which includes anticipated improvements.

18. Is a Pre-Approval Necessary for Real Estate Investment Loans?

While not always required, a pre-approval offers several advantages:

- Competitive Advantage: Sellers prefer buyers with pre-approvals as it shows financing readiness.
- Clear Budget: Pre-approval gives investors a clearer understanding of how much they can borrow, helping them focus on suitable properties.

Real estate financing encompasses a broad spectrum of loans and considerations tailored to various investment strategies and financial profiles. By understanding the answers to these frequently asked questions, investors can better navigate the complexities of financing, select suitable loan products, and make informed decisions that align with their investment goals. The knowledge provided here serves as a foundation for successful real estate investing and efficient portfolio management.

Investment Loans Checklist

Loan Type	Property Types	Down Payment	Credit Score	Income Verification	Special Requirements
Conventional	Residential up to 4 units	15-25%	620+	W-2s, tax returns	DTI < 45%, 6-12 months reserves
FHA	Up to 4 units, owner-occupied	3.5%	580+	W-2s, tax returns	MIP, must live in one unit
DSCR	Income-producing properties	20-30%	620+	Lease for rental income	DSCR > 1.25
Hard Money	Fix-and-flip properties	10-25%	600+	Rehab plan, exit strategy	Short term, high rates
Commercial	Multi-family (5+), office, retail	20-30%	660+	Property income statements	DSCR > 1.25, appraisal, environmental review
Bridge	Distressed, undervalued	15-30%	Flexible	Collateral	Short term, exit strategy required
Bank Statement	Residential, small commercial	10-25%	620+	12-24 months bank statements	Self-employed, no tax returns needed
Private Loan	Any, incl. unconventional	10-30%	Flexible	Flexible	Collateral, possibly higher down payment or assets as backup

This checklist can help you to quickly identify the type of financing that aligns with your property and investment goals and ensure you meet the requirements for a smoother loan approval process.

Building Your Real Estate Investment Financing Strategy

Building a real estate investment strategy requires careful planning, research, and a deep understanding of financing options. Successful investors use their financing strategically to expand their portfolios, maximize returns, and mitigate risks. This final chapter will guide you through the essential steps of developing a financing strategy tailored to your investment goals, financial situation, and risk tolerance.

1. Set Clear Investment Goals

The first step to a successful real estate investment financing strategy is defining your goals. Consider questions like:

- **What are your short-term and long-term goals?** Are you looking for quick returns through flips, or are you focused on building a portfolio of rental properties for steady cash flow and long-term appreciation?
- **What types of properties are you interested in?** The financing options for residential, multi-family, and commercial properties vary greatly, so knowing your focus will guide your loan choices.
- **What is your desired level of involvement?** For instance, a buy-and-hold strategy typically requires long-term management and property upkeep, while fix-and-flip properties involve more intense, short-term commitments.

By setting specific goals, you can align your financing choices to support your investment journey.

Building Your Real Estate Investment Financing Strategy

2. Assess Your Financial Position

Understanding your financial position is crucial before pursuing investment financing. Factors to assess include:

- **Credit Score:** Many lenders use your credit score to determine loan eligibility and interest rates. Improving your score can unlock more favorable terms, making a significant difference in long-term returns.
- **Savings and Capital:** Calculate how much you can allocate toward down payments, closing costs, and emergency reserves. Real estate investments often require a larger upfront commitment than personal home purchases, so ensuring adequate capital is key.
- **Debt-to-Income Ratio (DTI):** Lenders use DTI to assess how much debt you can comfortably handle. Higher debt loads can impact your ability to qualify for new loans, so managing your existing debt is essential.
- **Cash Flow Needs:** Determine your cash flow goals to balance debt obligations with your desired income from rental properties. This assessment will guide the financing structure that best supports your cash flow requirements.

3. Choose the Right Financing Options

Selecting the financing type that aligns with your strategy and property type is a cornerstone of your investment plan. Here's a quick guide based on different strategies:

- **For Rental Properties:** Consider conventional loans, DSCR loans, or FHA loans (if you're living in one unit of a multi-family property). These options provide stability and support long-term cash flow.
- **For Fix-and-Flip Projects:** Short-term financing options like hard money loans or bridge loans allow for rapid access to capital, helping you secure, renovate, and sell properties quickly.
- **For Multi-Family Properties:** Commercial real estate loans or DSCR loans are often ideal for multi-family investments, as these loans are tailored to income-generating properties.
- **For Self-Directed Retirement Funds:** Investors with self-directed IRAs or 401(k)s may explore real estate as an investment, though it's critical to follow IRS rules closely.

Your financing choice impacts everything from cash flow to tax implications, so research loan types and talk to lenders to determine the most suitable products for your strategy.

Building Your Real Estate Investment Financing Strategy

4. Optimize Your Loan Structure for Growth

As your portfolio grows, your financing needs may change. Here are key strategies to optimize financing at different stages:

- **Leverage Equity for Additional Investments:** If you have equity in your properties, consider refinancing or taking out a home equity loan to free up funds for future purchases.
- **Consider Portfolio Loans:** When you own multiple properties, some lenders offer portfolio loans, which bundle several mortgages under one loan. This approach simplifies management and can help secure favorable terms across all properties.
- **Utilize Cash-Out Refinancing:** Cash-out refinancing can be a powerful tool for extracting equity from existing properties to fund new acquisitions, renovations, or other investment opportunities.
- **Focus on Cash Flow–Positive Investments:** For long-term growth, prioritize properties that are cash flow positive after expenses. This approach provides financial stability, enabling you to cover mortgage payments, maintenance, and other expenses without dipping into personal funds.

5. Monitor Market Conditions and Adjust Accordingly

Real estate markets fluctuate, and strategic investors adapt their plans based on market trends:

- **Adjust Your Leverage During Market Highs**: During periods of market appreciation, consider cash-out refinancing or selling properties at peak values to maximize your returns.
- **Seek Low-Interest Opportunities in Downturns:** When interest rates are low, refinancing existing properties or securing additional loans can lower your overall debt costs and increase your cash flow.
- **Focus on Properties with Long-Term Value:** If markets experience a downturn, holding onto properties with strong long-term rental potential can provide income stability and protect you from short-term market volatility.

Regularly reviewing your strategy and adapting to market shifts can increase your resilience to economic changes.

Building Your Real Estate Investment Financing Strategy

6. Implement Sound Risk Management Practices

Risk management is essential to ensure sustainable growth and protect your investment. Here's how to manage financing risks effectively:

- **Maintain Emergency Funds:** Keep reserves for vacancies, unexpected repairs, and market downturns. Having access to emergency funds can help prevent financial strain.
- **Avoid Overleveraging:** Borrowing too much relative to your cash flow can lead to financial difficulties, especially during market downturns. Aim to keep your LTV (loan-to-value) ratio within a comfortable range, balancing growth with manageable debt.
- **Diversify Your Investment Portfolio:** Expanding your portfolio across different property types and locations reduces dependency on a single asset, which can lower risk.
- **Secure Insurance:** Ensure each property is well-insured, and consider adding liability protection to mitigate risk from potential lawsuits or property damage.

7. Build Strong Relationships with Lenders

Your relationship with lenders can make a significant difference in your investment success. Here are tips for establishing strong lender relationships:

- **Communicate Regularly:** Keep your lender informed of any changes in your financial situation or portfolio. Open communication fosters trust and can help expedite future loan applications.
- **Work with Specialized Lenders:** Many lenders specialize in real estate investment financing and understand unique investor needs, offering more flexibility and tailored products.
- **Negotiate Terms:** Don't hesitate to negotiate interest rates, points, and fees. Experienced lenders may be open to adjustments, especially if you're a long-term client.

Building a reputation as a reliable borrower can open doors to more favorable financing opportunities as you expand your portfolio.

Building Your Real Estate Investment Financing Strategy

8. Build a Team of Financial Experts

Investing in real estate requires a network of skilled professionals, including:

- **Mortgage Brokers:** They can help find the best loan options tailored to your investment goals.
- **Real Estate Attorneys:** Essential for navigating legal issues, especially with complex commercial or multi-family properties.
- **Accountants:** Tax planning is critical in real estate investing; an accountant can ensure you're leveraging all tax benefits.
- **Property Managers:** For large portfolios, property managers streamline operations and maintain property quality, making it easier to focus on growth.

Having a strong team increases your confidence in making sound financial decisions and enables a smoother path to scaling your investments.

Your Path to Real Estate Investment Success

Building a real estate investment financing strategy is about aligning your financial resources, goals, and market knowledge into a cohesive plan. This journey requires continual learning and flexibility to adapt to market conditions, financing trends, and personal growth as an investor.

Every investment will teach you something new. Whether you're starting with a single-family rental or branching into multi-family or commercial real estate, a clear financing strategy enables you to make informed decisions, mitigate risks, and steadily grow your portfolio. With the knowledge from this book, you're equipped to evaluate opportunities confidently, secure the right financing, and take actionable steps toward building long-term wealth through real estate.

Final Thoughts from the Author

Thank you for joining me on this journey through the world of real estate investment financing. As you've seen, successful investing isn't just about the properties you buy but also the strategies you use to finance them. With the right knowledge, planning, and a willingness to adapt, you have the power to turn real estate into a robust vehicle for wealth and financial freedom.

Whether you're just starting or looking to expand an established portfolio, remember that every investment decision shapes your path forward. Keep learning, stay curious, and don't hesitate to reach out to experienced professionals who can guide and support you along the way. I hope this book provides a foundation that empowers you to make informed choices and take confident steps toward achieving your financial dreams.

- STACY ANN STEPHENS